Go
and Sin
No more

The Power of
a Second Chance
from God through
Jesus Christ

Getchens Mathurin

innovo
PUBLISHING
innovopublishing.com

Published by Innovo Publishing, LLC
www.innovopublishing.com
1-888-546-2111

innovo
PUBLISHING
innovopublishing.com

Publishing Books, eBooks, Audiobooks, Music, Screenplays, & Courses for the
Christian & wholesome markets since 2008.

GO, AND SIN NO MORE
The Power of a Second Chance from God through Jesus Christ

Library of Congress Control Number: 2023916324
ISBN: 978-1-61314-952-2

Cover Design & Interior Layout: Innovo Publishing, LLC

Printed in the United States of America
U.S. Printing History
First Edition: 2023

This book is dedicated to those who are in need of another chance from God in one or many aspects of their lives.

Contents

Introduction

When Jesus had lifted up Himself, and saw none but the woman, He said unto her, Woman, where are those thine accusers? Hath no man condemned thee? She said, No man, Lord. And Jesus said unto her, Neither do I condemn thee: go, and sin no more. (John 8:10-11)

Lost through so many illusions coming from our weak human nature and countless dark forces around us, we often don't think in a pure way, fail to do justly, and fall short in speaking words conceived by wisdom. The laws, principles, customs, and time in which we are living often call for our death. Our moral death. Our psychological death. Our spiritual death. Our emotional death. There are so many ways to die. Multiple manners to expire. Infinite paths to step into eternity.

Society and its laws judge us based upon what they have established as values and morality, which makes sense in so many aspects because any community must define the core of each principle that its members should abide by. When Jesus asked the woman "if no one condemn you," we see the idea of a trial—if not formal, at least informal—like would later be the case for Jesus Himself before Pontius Pilate.

The severity of capital punishment could be a subject of great disagreement as it involves taking away someone's life. A death sentence is irreversible given that, if new data emerges later in favor of the deceased, they can't be brought back to life. No judicial system can bring back a condemned individual who was beheaded or hanged, according to the old practices, or one whose blood has been invaded by a mortal poison following a proposed civil death of the present age. Victor Hugo, one of the greatest writers of all time, vehemently opposed capital punishment. His reflection in his book *The Last Day of a Condemned Man,*[1] which is a plea for the abolishment of capital punishment, is to be read with scrutiny.

The death sentence seems to be as old as the world itself. The Mosaic Law prescribed death following so many violations, such as adultery. Yes, it is in the Bible—in the Old Covenant, to be exact—but the substance of the law could sometimes be very controversial. What should the law accomplish at the end? One answer is to keep a member of society from doing bad. The ethical question each society faces is, *What is bad and what is good?* Each religion tries to draw lines between good and bad, right and wrong. It is a great source of moral confusion to willfully interchange good and bad, even to do so innocently. The Bible says, "Woe unto them that call evil good and good evil; that put darkness for light, and light for darkness; that put bitter for sweet, and sweet for bitter!" (Isaiah 5:20).

The objective of the law is also to keep the sin nature of man under control via punishment. This is surely the purpose of the Mosaic Law. Speaking with the Church of Galatia, the Apostle Paul wrote, "Wherefore then serveth the Law? It was added because of transgressions" (Galatians 3:19). Coming back from slavery, the people of Israel under the leadership of Moses have seen a powerful manifestation of God through miracles like the death of the first male born of all Egyptian families while the first sons of Israel's households were exempt at Goshen. The literal crossing of the Red Sea was also remarkable, among other wonders. But still the Israelites complained in the wilderness because they

---

1. Victor Hugo, *The Last Day of a Condemned Man.* France: Gosselin, 1829.

were hungry and thirsty, and they wished they had stayed in Egypt since at least water and food had been at their disposal. It was like turning the omnipotent God into a toy god who cannot see and a heartless father who doesn't care about His children, the kind of god who is far away and cannot listen to the call of his servants. Consider Elijah, the prophet of God, who challenged the false prophets of Baal. God heard his cry and would bring fire to the sacrifice on the altar (1 Kings 18:20-40). We can then understand why the living God, as a good and capable Father, would be mad at the descendants of Jacob who likely had a memory problem and, consequently, always seemed to forget what God had done before.

The Mosaic Law is a form of punishment in the sense that it was a heavy burden the people of Israel couldn't bear in any way. As a child, following some of my misbehaviors, my mother would ask me to stand on one foot for an extended period. She surely knew I wouldn't be able to do this for as long as she required because of the pressure it placed on my standing foot. It hurt! God gives us two feet for a good reason, but when a Caribbean mother asks you to use only one as a punishment for wrongdoing, you do it. And it's hard!

First, I will address the question of fairness following a violation of a law—like stoning a woman who commits adultery but not a man. As Christians, we should rather call for forgiveness. It is hard to explain why death was the punishment for so many sins in the Old Covenant, but this was what God prescribed at that point in time, and we must accept it. The Apostle Paul teaches us that "The law is holy" (Romans 7:12). It was given by God Himself and is a mirror to look upon. I also believe the Old Covenant was written in a specific cultural and religious context. It is difficult for us, as products of a liberal time and living in America in the twenty-first century, to fully understand the fairness of this law. How many of us today would look at this statute with disgrace, contesting this law with all the freedoms that our now-democratic society offers to women? Time has evolved. Women are seen now with more humanity and are given more control over their body and the choices they make. But in so many countries and in so many cultures, women are still held to these old laws involving adultery.

As it relates to fairness, others might point out the discrimination of a law that underlines the punishment for a guilty woman, while no reprimand is given to the faulty man, even though the act was committed by both of them. The truth is, this unfortunate woman was living in a male-dominated society where even a firstborn male seemed to have more value than the mother herself when it comes to role and privilege in society. It is sad to state it, but it is the truth. In this sense it is worth noting how Jesus contributed greatly to the emancipation of women and could, in my view, be considered a pioneer of feminism.

Second, throughout this book, I will reflect on the adulterous woman from John 8, who was caught in the act of adultery under the Mosaic Law. Jesus already taught in an unconventional way. His preaching in the Sermon on the Mount reported in Matthew 5 underlined the contrast of so many instructions between the Old and New Covenants. This sermon portrayed the moral teaching of Jesus that would later constitute the essence of the new era known as the dispensation of grace or the age of the church.

Third, in correlation with the faulty woman will stand Richardson,[2] a young man who, after being a faithful servant of the Lord, endured many spiritually dark phases in his life where another chance from God became necessary. With astonishment, some neighbors who knew Richardson before observed his change in behavior and expected fire to fall from the sky onto him as divine justice.

---

2. Pseudonym. Any resemblance with a real person who exists or has existed is purely coincidental.

Those who brought the promiscuous woman to the Messiah imagined He would blame the sinner using the choicest corrective words. They might even have expected the Son of God to join them in throwing stones in complete fury. But the coming of the Lord Jesus inaugurated the season of grace, as He clearly introduced to the Pharisees through His Sabbath reading in the synagogue, narrated in the Gospel of Luke: "The Spirit of the Lord is upon me because he has anointed me. . . . to proclaim the year of the Lord's favor" (Luke 4:18-19 NIV).

Jesus came not to condemn but to give life abundantly. He came to give another chance to this unfaithful woman, to Richardson . . . to Zacchaeus the chief tax collector, to the prostitute who washed His feet with her tears and dried them with her hair, to the prodigal son who went far away from his father, to you and me. He came to say to all of us sinners who fall short of the glory of God, "Go, and sin no more" (John 8:11).

1

Adultery in the Old Covenant

A dultery is the act of infidelity between one or more married individuals. It is prohibited by the seventh of the Ten Commandments, which simply says, "You shall not commit adultery" (Exodus 20:12). One might ask to whom this command was verily or mainly addressed? A curious soul might question who was likely to get caught in the act of adultery. An inquisitive mind would likely observe that the definition is misogynistic since the object of the definition often refers only to a married woman. The truth is, at this time, the Jewish community revolved around a male-value approach. In this era, a married man being intimate with an unmarried woman was not technically adultery under the Jewish law.

The command in the book of Leviticus, "Moreover thou shalt not lie carnally with thy neighbor's wife, to defile thyself with her" (Leviticus 18:20), has often been a recourse to state that the act of adultery for a man is established even in the case where the faulty woman is unmarried. However, it is not a difficult point to make that men in the Old Covenant often had a multitude of unmarried women. The problem with David sleeping with Bathsheba was that she was a married woman. Her husband, at the same time, was fighting in the Israeli army at war against a national enemy. It may be permissible to say that David was often seen more as a murderer than as an adulterer. That the king was more an unfair man than an immoral one. He was the one who took the only little ewe lamb from a poor man to feed his guests while he already owned so many in his backyard—to paraphrase the wise word of the prophet Nathan, who was sent by God to rebuke David's actions (2 Samuel 2:1–4).

In a similar light, King Solomon's mess with his thousand wives and concubines was mostly because of where they came from—those countries where God explicitly said to Moses,

> Neither shalt thou make marriages with [the Hittites, and the Girgashites, and the Amorites, and the Canaanites, and the Perizzites, and the Hivites, and the Jebusites]; thy daughter thou shalt not give unto his son, nor his daughter shalt thou take unto thy son. For they will turn away thy son from following me, that they may serve other gods; so will the anger of the LORD be kindled against you, and destroy thee suddenly. (Deuteronomy 7:3-4)

Effectively, the son of David turned away from God thereafter because of those strangers' wives, who incited him to go after other gods. For that, Solomon can be viewed more as a spiritual fornicator than an adulterer. He could be perceived as a disobedient king rather than one who could not turn his eyes from beautiful women, no matter where they came from.

In a similar way, the Apostle Paul wrote to the Corinthian churches, "Be ye not yoked together with unbelievers: for what fellowship hath righteousness and unrighteousness? And what communion hath light with darkness?" (2 Corinthians 6:14).

Brothers and sisters, when God gives His people a commandment, He knows exactly why. When God speaks to the Church in a specific way, there is a valid reason. Every command has value in the eyes of our Lord—even the ones that appear to be so simple. God *cannot* speak in vain. Wisdom pours from His words. We may have difficulty comprehending this sometimes, but illumination from above will open our eyes at last. How many of us suffer because we simply ignore God's commandments?

Today, the people of God, the Church—which doesn't replace the people of Israel because Israel will always be the people of God—come from all nations, and the strangers would be those who do not accept Jesus Christ as their Lord and Savior. Remember Jesus says, "I am the light of the world" (John 8:12). And Paul asked the Corinthian Church, "What communion hath light with darkness?" (2 Corinthians 6:14).

As a Christian, a man can marry any woman from another nation as long as she is in Christ. As a follower of Jesus, a woman can marry any man from another nation as long as she knows Jesus as Savior. This is the fundamental aspect of the sanctity of our Christian marriages. That's why a woman can still connect with her husband while he is far away for a long time. Marriage is more than just a physical relationship—it is spiritual and emotional. If there is no emotion or feeling between a man and a woman as a couple, then the physical or intimate aspect is meaningless.

The human body could be viewed simply as a body of a tree: both have life and will die someday. Some, for example, even agree to give their body to a stranger for money. But they never give their heart. They keep their mouths closed during the interaction because a woman's mouth is the fundamental gate to her soul. When a woman kisses a man, she gives him a considerable fraction of her heart. But a prostitute who does not kiss a stranger maintains a hold on her feelings.

Eros is a wonderful feeling. Loving someone unconditionally is divine. It is so true that sometimes we don't understand why exactly a husband loves his wife. We cannot comprehend why this woman loves her husband so much: no physical appeal, no wealth, no fame, nothing. This is unconditional love.

When you confess your faith and prioritize it, an unsaved spouse might feel estranged from your life. Religion is a daily habit, a continual behavior that you openly express and intimately carry. Imagine a woman keeps repeating the name of Jesus, to which her husband is a complete stranger. Some men surely grow annoyed at this, and some might ask for a break. A more moderate man might keep silent. In any case, the couple faces harm. It is a great risk for a Christian to marry an unbeliever, and it often leads to moral confusion. A Christian woman might ask her husband to go to a church service at night while he proposes a nightclub program instead. Each spouse has two different states of mind, two different ways to see the world—and two different sets of words to write about it. Most of the time, the husband prevails because he must be the head of the household.

Some women think they can try hard to take their unbelieving fiancé to church. *If he truly loves me, then he will try to please me and God will do the rest*, they imagine. I know God sometimes acts in mysterious ways, but if we disobey God's command about such an important and consequential matter, what we can expect but all kinds of problems? Some women try to pave the way by saying, *I'm going to change him by my exemplary lifestyle.* It is true that a wife with virtue could be influential, but it may be not enough to turn her unconverted spouse into a Christian. Remember we do not have enough spiritual resources within to change ourselves and, indeed, we cannot pretend we can change someone else. Only the Holy Spirit can transform someone with that person's goodwill.

If you are a man or woman of God who has an unsaved spouse, you still can ask God for another chance. You can still fall to your knees and ask God for forgiveness. Repeat this prayer:

> *Dear God!*
>
> *I disobeyed your command that forbids me to marry an unbeliever, and I'm so sorry. I pray that you build what I cannot build; I pray that you open the doors I cannot open; I pray that you give me another chance with your Word as a lamp unto my feet, as Psalm 119:105 says.*

I don't know exactly how God is going to answer your prayer, but I do know He is the God of second chances.

To you, young Christian who is ready to get married, please be sure that your soon-to-be- spouse knows about Jesus. Do not disobey the Word of God, which asks you not to ally yourself with unfaithful people. You might be their friend, coworker, or adviser—but not a husband or a wife. Don't put yourself in a position where even the name of Jesus is barely allowed to be repeated inside your home, and avoid a situation where you have to give your spouse money just to attend a church service once a year. Even if your spouse miraculously accepts, when attending the service you may still feel as if he or she were coming from another planet.

Try to control your feelings, young woman! Just because you love a man doesn't mean you have to marry him, even if he kneels with a ring or sends you flowers like a scene from a romance movie. Life sometimes seems like a theater where we simply play our role. But when we return to reality, many of us find that it's too late to take back control of our situation.

Try to control your feelings, young man! Just because you fall in love with a woman doesn't mean you have to marry her at any price, even if she is beautiful like the Shulamite (Song of Solomon 6:13). Before deciding to marry someone, you need to look at several criteria. To love and be loved, for example, is an important one. It is not wise to fall in love today and plan to marry a few days later without involving any family or friends. We forget so many times that, at a certain level, our life belongs not only to ourselves but to our loved ones and friends. The people who are part of our existence help us to have better days in this complex reality called life, and our decisions affect them, too. No one lives completely for him or herself, and no one dies entirely alone.

You need some time to know the person you love. You need some time to see how your fiancé reacts when he or she is angry. A person's real character is mostly expressed during trouble. You need some time to test your relationship. You need to go meet his or her family. As a man, you need to observe how your girlfriend speaks to her father and brothers. As a woman, you need to examine how your boyfriend talks to his mother and sisters. It might reflect the reality to come once you are married. Two or three meetings in a restaurant plus some rendezvous at your favorite movie theater aren't enough to know your relationship. Even the workplace in which you both spend a lot of time is still not enough to discover someone's true personality.

Although we recognize how difficult it is to know someone this well, experiencing the real person you are going to marry is beneficial. Today you might not even be sure whether the beautiful face you see is a fake one made with plastic. On your honeymoon, you even might be surprised as a happy, newly married man to see your wife not only take off her clothes but display other things that could make you run away trembling or call for help.

God is the only one who knows each of us in our entirety: body, soul, and heart. Because of that, as a Christian, you need time to let God know about your decision to marry someone. Invite God into your marriage because you never know when the wine will run out! Invite God into your journey because He might give you some signs that would help you weigh this important decision. He could also tell you openly. God can help you find a faithful, loving spouse who is ready to take the way of salvation with you. There are so many good things in the house of the Lord. Do not fear that God might force you to marry someone for whom you do not have any feeling. God is not a dictator. He knows about your erotic love and respects it because He was the one who created you and put it in you. The Bible says: "Delight thyself also in the LORD: and He shall give thee the desires of thine heart" (Psalm 37:4). God knows what is good for you while taking into consideration your own feelings. Do not compromise your faith if you believe a divorce would hurt you considerably.

Remember when a family falls apart, when divorce comes to the equation, unhappiness and even depression often follow somehow. There are many ways for a family to be unhappy, like the great Russian writer Leo Tolstoy nicely expressed it in his time: "All happy families are alike but every unhappy family is unhappy in its own way."[3] I can't count the number of Christian brothers and sisters I personally know who have suffered because of their horrible decision to marry an unbeliever. If I had five hands, I still wouldn't be able to count them all. It is better to be careful than to ask God for another chance.

---

3. Leo Tolstoy, *Anna Karenina,* 1st ed., Sterling, 2012.

Polygamy wasn't prohibited in the Old Covenant. Having multiple wives wasn't considered an act of adultery, but a married woman could not have an affair with someone other than her spouse. If a man under the Mosaic Law had enough financial resources, felt attracted to more than one woman, and/or reasoned that it was the right thing to do, nothing refrained him from having multiple wives. Elkanah, a good servant of the Lord, had two spouses, Hannah and Peninnah. Unfortunately—or, for some men, fortunately—polygamy is still accepted and practiced in some places around the world. Many even believe that if a man is aware of his sexual desire, his true tendency is to have multiple lovers, as if being a conqueror of women is a sign of masculinity.

The Bible teaches us: "The fear of the LORD is the beginning of wisdom" (Proverbs 9:10). The New Covenant doesn't teach that a man can marry multiple women or can marry one and have multiple mistresses. To the Corinthian Church, Apostle Paul said, "Now concerning the things whereof ye wrote unto me: It is good for a man not to touch a woman. Nevertheless, to avoid fornication, let every man have his own wife, and let every woman have her own husband" (1 Corinthians 7:1–2). The confusion and rivalry polygamy causes among wives has never been part of God's plan. At the beginning, He created Adam and Eve as man and wife (Genesis 3:6). He could have created two or three women for Adam, but He did not. The first instance of polygamy in the Bible, Lamech taking two wives, shows how inclined we are toward sin (Genesis 4:19). Because of their disobedience to the Lord, many Israelites were killed in military service. The more men died, the more Israelites began to perceive polygamy as acceptable and even necessary.

Luckily the Occident embraced Christianity, which teaches that a man and a woman—and eventually their kids—make up a family. This view follows the original teaching in the New Covenant and avoids many problems.

A Christian man who respects God and His commands should not have secret wives or mistresses. He knows that a man can hide from his wife but not from God. The same goes for a Christian woman. Like the psalmist expressed, God's eyes are upon us all day long: "If I ascend up into heaven, thou art there: if I make my bed in hell, behold, thou art there" (Psalm 139:8).

My point is not that a Christian is as pure as Mary the mother of Jesus while an unbeliever is a sinner like Barabbas. My position is not that Christians and non-Christians are two worlds without any similarity. At the end of the day, both share the same human condition and both are under the influence of inherited sin. Everybody sins, Christian and non-Christian. The Bible says, "For all have sinned, and come short of the glory of God" (Romans 3:23). Not "some have sinned" but "all."

The Holy Spirit works within us, and the fear of the Lord flourishes to keep us from crossing certain lines like polygamy, which is practiced in the Old Covenant and in some parts of the world today. Adultery in the Old Covenant shows how sexist the Jewish society was and how inequality between man and woman can be discriminatory toward the latter.

2

Adultery in the New Covenant

Ye have heard that it was said by them of old time, Thou shall not commit adultery: But I say unto you, That whosoever looketh on a woman to lust after her hath committed adultery with her already in his heart. (Matthew 5:27–28)

There are so many ways in which the Old Covenant is different from the new one. One of them is that the Mosaic Law, The Torah, was demonstrative while the grace of the New Covenant is more spiritual: an intimate relationship with God via His Son, Jesus Christ, by faith. The Mosaic Laws were mainly applicable for ceremonial duties. The priest and other people working in the temple had to be careful when using items meant for serving God. They had to be careful with their procedures. They also had to go to a specific place of worship, like the Samaritan lady mentioned when she reminded Jesus, "Our fathers worshipped in this mountain; and Ye say, that in Jerusalem is the place where men ought to worship. Jesus saith unto her, Woman, believe me, the hour cometh, when ye shall neither in this mountain, nor yet at

Jerusalem, worship the Father. Ye worship ye know not what: we know what we worship: for salvation is of the Jews" (John 4:20–22).

In the Old Testament, what happened in the mind did not matter as much as the act of sin. If I saw a woman and imagined being intimate with her, it wouldn't be cause for remorse. A married woman would not have been stoned for imagining herself in bed with another lover since no one has access to her thoughts. But in the New Covenant, the Word of God emphasizes what happens inside our hearts. Our Lord cares if we keep it pure or not, and our relationship with Him starts there.

In the Sermon on the Mount, Jesus said that the act of adultery starts in the mind, contrary to the old view that thoughts were only sinful when acted upon (Matthew 5:27–28). According to the new dispensation, a man does not have to lay down in a bed with a woman for adultery to be committed. The Mosaic Law was about what the people of Israel did and what the leaders could see, but with the New Covenant, God sees our mischief and underlines it at its start: our spirit. That is why a Christian must carefully follow this wise advice from Solomon, the teacher: "Keep thy heart with all diligence; for out of it are the issues of life" (Proverbs 4:23). Jesus elaborated on this matter:

> Not that which goeth into the mouth defileth a man; but that which cometh out of the mouth, this defileth a man. . . . But those things which proceed out of the mouth come forth from the heart; and they defile the man. For out of the heart proceed evil thoughts, murders, adulteries, fornications, thefts, false witness, blasphemies. (Matthew 15:11–19)

While praying, we often ask God to forgive the sins we commit via our actions, our words, and our mind. As Christians, we are not allowed to use our imagination in a sinful way, even if it's impossible for us to act on that thought. It is a difficult exercise to be careful with what we see and process in our mind. I'm not saying it is easy. Sometimes we go so far just to follow a glance. It is our responsibility to do our best to take care of our imagination.

If there was nothing you could have done about the first glance, try to avoid the second one. Try to fix your imagination on what God has done for you and what He is about to do. Focus on your dream: the bachelor's degree you want to finish or the master's you contemplate in your mind. How to succeed with your business. How to make money in the stock market with your financial knowledge and the illumination of the Holy Spirit. Bad thinking will surely come, but we will fight them with our conviction and the help of the Holy Spirit. As Martin Luther famously said, "You cannot keep birds from flying over your head, but you can keep them from building a nest in your hair."[4]

As a Christian, if you feel you use your imagination to do anything, you are wrong and need another chance from God to focus on what is positive intellectually and pure spiritually. I have no better recommendation other than the one apostle Paul gave to the Church of Philippi at the conclusion of his letter: "Finally, brothers and sisters, whatever is true, whatever is noble, whatever is right, whatever is pure, whatever is lovely, whatever is admirable— if anything is excellent or praiseworthy—think about such things" (Philippians 4:8 NIV).

---

4. Martin Luther, "Explanation of the Lord's Prayer." In *Large Catechism*. Wittenberg: 1529.

3

Jesus as a Pioneer of Feminism

F eminist" could be defined an infinite number of ways. I do not embrace political approaches that describe "feminist" as "a range of social-political movement and ideologies that aims to define and establish the political, economic, personal, and social equality of the sexes."[5] This definition is too vague and, consequently, dangerous. For Christians, being feminist doesn't mean wanting man to be equal to woman in all aspects, nor does it mean wanting a man to be transformed into a woman or vice versa. Feminism doesn't mean a woman must do anything that a man can do, especially since it is evident that man and woman are different biologically and emotionally. The German philosopher Friedrich Nietzsche stated, "Man is superior to woman when it comes to reason while woman is superior to man when it comes to emotion."[6] A man is naturally stronger than a woman, although exceptions exist where some women are strong and some men are weak.

5. Chris Beasley, *What is Feminism?* New York: Sage, 1999.
6. Friedrich Nietzsche, *Joyful Science*, Berlin: Berlin House of Authors, 1885.

In this book, I adopt a view that defines feminism as "The belief that women should be allowed the same right, power and opportunities as men and be treated in the same ways, or the set of activities intended to achieve this state."[7]

Women's duties were mostly domestic across history in many societies, including Jewish culture. Notably, Middle Eastern culture at large was male dominant at the time. Women were second-class citizens with very few rights. If you carefully read the books of the Old Testament, you will realize that women were scarcely present in social and political spheres. However, it is worth remembering that one female—the only one to be called a judge and a prophet, and the only one to perform a judicial function—was Deborah (Judges 5). Somehow the public service wasn't totally closed to women, and Deborah's role reminded all women that they could become whatever they wish. A judge or a lawyer, a president or a senator, an engineer or a doctor, a CEO or a banker—as time passed, the gate of profession swung open and some nonsense customs became obsolete. Thank God. But it was a hard lesson for many sexists who believe a woman should stay at home to take care of domestic affairs, including educating their kids.

At the beginning of His ministry, Jesus chose His disciples. Although His intimate circle, the twelve, included only men, some of his followers were women. Still, many observers were amazed that women were so close to Jesus, some having been given valuable duties. Jesus saw women as equal to men and treated them with mutual respect. At this time, Jesus was revolutionary when it comes to His behavior toward women. For example, Jesus was the first to start the conversation during his encounter with the Samaritan

---

7. *Cambridge English Dictionary*, Cambridge: Cambridge University Press, 1995.

woman, knowing that Jewish tradition dictated a respectable man should not speak to a woman he did not know.

Jesus also put His commitments to practice. He engaged with so many women, among them an elderly woman whose only son crossed the gate of eternity. Another one was a prostitute who came uninvited to a rich man's dinner, where she washed Jesus' feet with her tears. He did not push her away, as the host and other guests expected.

What about the woman caught in the act of adultery? Jesus might ask why they brought only her. He might look at a human being degraded by the stronger of the two genders. He surely saw someone who committed a mistake like the other person involved did, yet both people were equally wrong and in need of God's forgiveness. Socioeconomic unfairness toward women is one of the reasons we call for the feminist movement all around the world, in the Middle East or in Europe, in America or in Africa.

Jesus befriended Mary and Martha and their brother Lazarus. He surely saw the same moral standard and strong character in the two sisters that He saw in their brother Lazarus. They had honorable values worthy of establishing a friendship with all three of them. Women were present around Jesus, and He cherished and empowered them the same way He did for His male disciples—in contrast to the time in which He was living. In this sense, He is a pioneer of feminism.

4

Another Chance for Your Drug Addiction

Richardson lay on his sofa in a fair-sized room, alone with his imagination. Things were in complete disorder: a plate of leftover food under his jacket, a bottle of juice close to an old Bible the young man no longer read, shoes to the left and sandals to the right. In the middle, a small puppy, who looked like he had never been washed, barked as if to say he was hungry and angry. The cloth sofa was extremely dirty, and the brown carpet was nearly unrecognizable because everything that had fallen on it had not been cleaned. From time to time, Richardson tasted a great amount of a substance white as flour, the same powder on his coffee table. He sometimes looked at the ceiling and at the wall in front of him, where a large, old picture of a lady with a traditional blue dress and a nice, big red hat hung. She always seemed to communicate something Richardson could barely understand. Intermittently, he answered the phone with kindness or anger while receiving instructions from a superior or giving directions to an inferior. In both cases, it was about a dirty activity: selling drugs.

Richardson was a thin, twenty-five-year-old black man. When he was younger, he was known as a very respectful young man to all—to adults and the elderly as well as to the young and adolescent. He was a kid when he was with other kids and an adult when with the adults. His arms were so often an extension for others, and his feet walked for so many in his community. Everyone loved him and enjoyed being with him. He was born in this neighborhood, and his mother was known as a fervent, Christian lady. She had taken her only son to church every Sunday morning and had shown him the way of salvation in Christ. The heart of this young man was in the right place, and under his mother's guidance, he demonstrated great devotion.

But life is fragile, and we live in a world where "the most beautiful things have often the worst destiny,"[8] to quote the French writer Francois Malherbe. On a Monday afternoon, the devoted lady was suddenly killed in an accident while coming back from a church meeting. A truck driver had lost control of his wheel and crashed into the small Chevrolet driven by Mrs. Johnson, who lost her life on impact. Richardson had been seated under a tree in front of his house, playing his guitar and singing a song he loved so much:

> *When peace like a river attendeth my way*
> *When sorrows like sea billows roll*
> *Whatever my lot, thou hast taught me to say:*
> *It is well; it is well with my soul.*[9]

It is simple to sing "it is well with my soul," but having this soul destroyed by the sudden passing of a loving mother

---

8. Francois Malherbe, *Consolations to Mr. Du Perier*, Guillemot Edition, Paris: 1607.

9. Horatio Gates Spafford, "It is Well with My Soul." In *Gospel Hymns No. 2*. Philadelphia: Ira Sankey and Bliss, 1878.

is a reality much more complex. When Richardson learned about the accident because of an indiscreet woman who did not know how to deliver the sad news, he ran no less than one mile, calling, "Mama! Mama! Mama!" Three strong men had to refrain him from hurting himself and from accessing the accident scene. Sister Laura, a good friend of his mother, had been busy planning her next daughter's wedding and couldn't meet with the victim this afternoon, and she took the unfortunate son into her home. But she was inconsolable to a point where her dress was wet with tears. What a somber day for Flora County! People cried so loudly that the adjacent neighborhood could hear it, so loudly that surely the dead below were informed and the angels above were touched. That afternoon, the clouds in the sky closed their eyes, the atmosphere became dark, and rain fell from the sky with fury. It was as if Mother Nature joined the sons of man in this concert of sorrow for the departure of a wonderful soul. The spiritual mother of all was unexpectedly gone. Mother Johnson, as everyone had called her, used to have spiritual advice for anyone who needed it. She had always found the appropriate Bible verse to encourage her neighbors.

Richardson had been twenty-two years old when his mother was killed. He tried to understand why God had not intervened. He could not explain why a woman who loved God so much and did everything the right way had lost her life so tragically. Some of us have been on Earth for many more years than this orphan and have acquired a lot of wisdom, but we still do not comprehend why God sometimes allows some of His servants to die so awfully. For example, Brother Stephen in the Bible was stoned while observing the glory of God according to his own words (Acts of Apostles 7:55–56). As Christians, the sky often looks empty or God seems distant, but this is only a false impression. God is still on His throne no matter what. We just cannot comprehend His nature and His plans. Who has known the Mind of the Lord?

Paul said it well in his wonderful doxology in the letter to the Roman Church: "Oh, the depth of the riches of the wisdom and knowledge of God! How unsearchable His judgments, and His paths beyond tracing out! 'Who has known the mind of the Lord? Or who has been His counselor?' 'Who has ever given to God, that God should repay them?' For from Him and through Him and for Him are all things. To Him be the glory forever! Amen" (Romans 11:33–36 NIV).

Richardson hasn't been the same person since his mother went to the house of the Lord, the celestial home where suffering and death do not exist. *God has the power to save the author of my days, my lovely mother, from this terrible accident but chose not to do so*, he repeated in his heart. In the same way, God surely could have saved Stephen. *Why serve a God like that?* Richardson thought to himself. He knew how he could show his anger toward this omnipotent God: he would never pray or go to church again.

Pastor Andrew Deschamps tried his best to encourage the orphan to be at peace with life, God, and himself by using all resources available in the Bible and in the wisdom found in secular books, but the hill to climb was so high that his efforts were unsuccessful. The minister even fasted once a week for the return of the young man, but his words of consolation and those days of prayer seemed to be insufficient.

Overtime, Richardson distanced himself from the religious leader who had been his friend. He missed so many days of work without excuse and exhibited so many behavioral issues that he was fired. "Although we are very sorry for the passing of your mother and all the emotional troubles that followed, your position has been terminated as a result of your conduct. The young, intelligent man we hired and loved is long gone, and it is more advantageous for both parties to part ways, "stated a paragraph of the termination letter.

Richardson then became a member of the winning-by-all-means group, whose main occupation was selling drugs. He still tried to be respectful, but morally he was bankrupt. He was so dependent on drugs that a day couldn't pass by without taking a dose, as if it were a necessary medication his life depended on. People from his neighborhood could clearly see how bad his behaviors were. The young man they had known before disappeared like smoke.

He met his wife Linda the day he turned twenty-seven years old and married her one year later. His wife tried to make him reconcile with life, but the death of his mother had been too world-shattering and confusing for him. The faithful Christian lady tried to take him back to church, but Richardson had such bad habits with his strange friends that her attempt became too difficult. His heart had gone so far away from God. But in a spiritual bank account, someone made many deposits: a mother praying for her only son to remember there is a God, whatever the circumstances might be.

Like Richardson, many of us find refuge in drugs, alcohol, and smoking following the death of a loved one. We want God to understand that we are mad at Him and do not care about His laws anymore. It is so simple to just repeat in our local churches that "God is good all the time; all the time, God is good." But how meaningful are those words, verily! The death of a mother doesn't change who God is. The passing of a spouse doesn't alter God's fidelity. His justice endures eternally. We have to die because of what our ancestors Adam and Eve did in the Garden of Eden. No matter what happens in our life, God is still loving and good during hard times. Job learned this lesson in the hard way. All of his kids died, and he did not curse God, refuting a proposition his own wife had made (Job 2:9–10).

The good news is that God doesn't give up on us. He still has a project for each of his children, like He told the people of Israel amidst troubled times: "'For I know the plans I have for you,' declares the LORD, 'plans to prosper you and not to harm you, plans to give you hope and a future'" (Jeremiah 29:11 NIV). It is hard to understand why God allows a faithful servant to die, but we know that God always has a better plan. It is harmful when our loved ones pass away, but God is in control. When we suffer, it is wise sometimes to ask God to give us the strength to endure it. Life is equally unfair and imperfect for both believers and nonbelievers due to original sin, and sometimes we need spiritual energy from above since no one is exempt from this world's broken state. If the economy went into a recession, everyone would feel the impact. If the climate changes and the sea level rises too much, everyone would face consequences like flooding. Indeed, as a Christian, do not expect all problems to go away in order for God to be loving.

God wants to give you another chance. No more drugs, no more alcohol, and no more smoking. He wants to take you to the place where you used to be before; in fact, He wants to take you to an even better place. The passing of a loved one is surely a traumatic experience for each of us, and it is unfortunate that we have to go through the sad reality that is death. But we can feel relief and hope when we remember the death of a Christian is described as a sleep (1 Thessalonians 4:15–17). When we wake up, we will find ourselves in a wondrous place: in heaven, where there is no pain, no suffering, no corruption, and no separation from our loved ones.

5

Another Chance for Your Habitual, Sexual Sin

Richardson wasn't only addicted to drugs; he also became obsessed with using women to satisfy his passion. When we start doing wrong, we sometimes misbehave in many ways since one sin often leads to another. For example, in the book of Genesis, Cain was jealous of his brother Abel. He became a murderer, then became arrogant. "Am I my brother's keeper?" He answered God, who had asked him, "Where is your brother Abel?" (Genesis 4:9 NIV). In the book of Second Samuel, David committed adultery with Bathsheba and then carefully planned the murder of her spouse who, as an Israeli soldier, fought a nation enemy (2 Samuel 11).

Richardson swam in his river of transgression. He sometimes stopped to reflect how far he had gone and even shed some tears. After all, there is still a divine light within those who knew Christ before but had since strayed far. A guilty conscience can be a heavy weight to bear.

If you are under the influence of a sin, I want to remind you there is power in the blood of Jesus:

If you want to break all strings of sins
There is power in the blood of Jesus.

Richardson grew ashamed of himself. The picture of his mother on the wall became so unbearable to look at that he took it off. He felt he was on his way to perdition. He was destroying his body and his soul. He remembered the verse that his mother used to repeat to him: "Do you not know that your bodies are temples of the Holy Spirit, who is in you, whom you have received from God? You are not your own; you were bought at a price. Therefore honor God with your bodies" (1 Corinthians 6:19–20 NIV). One night, in a dream, he saw an angel of God standing in front of his bed. He told him that God wanted to give him another chance.

Like Richardson, so many of us—who had once been faithful servants in the house of the Lord—find ourselves trapped in a depraved life from which only God can rescue us. God is a God of second chances through His Son, Jesus Christ. He wants you to keep your body clean, pure from all sexual sins. He wants to help you to re-establish your body as the temple of the Holy Spirit.

Although we must have the will to leave behind this lifestyle, only the Holy Spirit can win over the bad sexual activities that have taken control of our minds. We do not have enough power to do it alone. The Bible says, "The heart is deceitful above all things and beyond cure. Who can understand it? I the LORD search the heart and examine the mind, to reward each person according to their conduct, according to what their deeds deserve" (Jeremiah 17:9–10 NIV). We naturally incline to do bad things because of our sinful nature. To the Ephesian Church, Apostle Paul expressed the same idea: "As for you, you were dead in your transgressions and sins, in which you used to live when you followed the ways of this world and of the ruler of the kingdom of the air, the spirit who is now at work in those who are disobedient" (Ephesians 2:1–2 NIV). A dead person cannot resurrect him or herself. That's why you must not think you can save yourself. You must ask God for help. He will be more than happy to come to the rescue, but He might not want to do it without you. Change your habits. Stop going to this nightclub where nude women flourish.

Sometimes we create our own problems. If I know my weaknesses, why do I put myself in a situation where I will be tempted to sin? If you have an alcohol problem, why is your bedroom full of rum and wine from the ceiling to the floor? Why do you enter a liquor store each time you pass by it? We must be wise because the battle we are in is a spiritual one. The devil knows us and does his best to push us away from God. Apostle Paul reminded the Ephesian Church, "For our struggle is not against flesh and blood, but against the rulers, against the authorities, against the powers of this dark work and against the spirituals forces of evil in the heavenly realms" (Ephesians 6:12 NIV). As I said before, it all starts in our hearts. Our misbehavior could stem from a bad, exterior influence, which is one interpretation of this verse. The prostitute you want to sleep with is not the problem, but the evil spirit that pushes you to do so is the real trouble. Remember, a long time ago God pushed Lucifer and his group of rebel angels from heaven because they invaded the spiritual sphere that Paul called "heavenly realms" (Isaiah 14: 12–15; Ephesians 6:12 NIV).

Our bad decisions mostly come from two sources. First is our corrupt human nature, as David clearly expressed it: "Surely I was sinful at birth, sinful from the time my mother conceived me" (Psalm 51:5 NIV). Apostle Paul also surprisingly stated, "As it is, it is no longer I myself who do it, but it is sin living in me" (Romans 7:17 NIV). I still remember being amazed when I first read this verse as a young Christian. Later, in theological seminar, I learned to distinguish between "inherited sin" and "actual sins" or "committed sins." Inherited sin refers to the sin nature inherited from our first parents, Adam and Eve. Actual sins refer to the transgressions we commit because of this depraved nature. The sin that Paul refers to in Roman 7:17–20 is inherited sin. The second source of our transgression is a bad influence coming from outside spiritual forces, like Paul clearly expressed in Ephesians 6:12.

Christ is our strength, and He is ready to be with us in our decision to return home. If you feel that you became a slave of sexual sin and need to give up your way of living, simply say this prayer:

> *Dear God,*
>
> *I'm sorry I have sinned. I ask you for forgiveness.*
>
> *I want to be free from all sexual sin; I want to be truly free. Come back into my heart. I want my body to be the temple of the Holy Spirit. I want it to be clean.*
>
> *I want to be yours eternally. Achieve what you already started in me a long time ago.*
>
> *In Jesus Christ I pray, amen!*

If you recite this prayer not only with your lips but also with your heart, I believe you will return to your Father and be born again. Find a good Christian church to attend. Ask God for direction. It is always good to be with our brothers and sisters in Christ. We find encouragement together, and we pray for each other.

6

Another Chance for Your Financial Failure

Richardson's mother believed every child is born with a specific intellectual gift that needs to be discovered and polished through education. When her only son was very young, she observed him sitting in front of the computer curiously, as if he was having a profound exchange with it. Later, when Richardson was only eleven years old, his mother didn't have to call Brother Peterson to fix her computer. That busy man needed an eternity to show up and most of the time couldn't do anything to resolve the problem.

Although she wasn't in a comfortable financial position, she did her best to push her beloved son to go to college, and even before he reached twenty-two years old, the young man had already finished a four-year degree in Computer and Technology. He had been offered a very well-paying job at a prestigious company and had become well respected. Many neighbors had been lucky enough to get their computer fixed by the humble and smart young man. Pastor Andrew, with whom he had developed a kind friendship, used to say, "Richardson speaks to a computer and it obeys; he touches it, and it's healed from all electronic illness."

Many times, our depravity comes with a great price. Richardson spent a lot of money to maintain his sinful lifestyle, but his friends did not care. They did not tell him to slow down. They did not warn him to seek a financial advisor. Instead, they pushed him to spend again and again and again. Somehow we often empty our pockets while turning our backs to our father—our biological father or our spiritual Father, our Lord.

The parable of the prodigal son, found in Chapter 15 of the Gospel according to Luke, expresses it well: "Not long after that, the younger son got together all he had, set off for a distant country and there squandered his wealth in wild living" (Luke 15:13 NIV). Oh, how ready we are to enjoy our lives as young people! Some of us choose to go far away to have the kind of life we want even if our parents are still alive. If our parents have already passed away, it's one less problem to face: we are free as the air. The prodigal son did not ask his father for a part of his inheritance—he wanted all of it. He was excited about his next trip and about what he would do away from his family. Again, this is our sin nature, this tendency to do bad things with ease. We often run toward transgression but slow down when, before us, the path of righteousness and wisdom opens.

If our foolishness appears to have no limits, our finances do. Spending in the morning without control, in the afternoon without thinking, and in the night without measure is a prelude to disaster and bankruptcy. No fortune is eternal; no wealth will endure forever while being used in a careless way.

Richardson used to take his friends to some nightclubs where alcohol flows like a river, capable of watering many acres of garden. In those places money is king—money is respect—because it is spent incessantly.

The prodigal son seemed to enjoy his life in a similar way, since the heart of man has stayed the same throughout time. "There is no new thing under the sun," to quote one of the wisest men who ever lived (Ecclesiastes 1:9). Indeed, history spins in repetitive orbit, with different faces doing things with the same heart and purpose: the supposed well-being of the human race.

Our money must first be used in a way that glorifies God. We must take care of ourselves by caring for our body, which is the temple of God. We can buy nice clothes, beautiful shoes, and luxurious jewels while we not becoming enslaved to them. We maintain our body's cleanliness in the same way evangelical leaders try to keep their churches clean for the service of the Lord.

Secondly, we also use our money for our academic education because it is a good way to acquire intelligence. In the book of Proverbs, Solomon gave instruction as a father: "Get wisdom, get understanding: forget it not; neither decline from the words of my mouth... Wisdom is the principal thing; therefore get wisdom: and with all thy getting get understanding" (Proverbs 4:5–7). There are two ways to define the word "wisdom." First, wisdom refers to prudence in the matters we are dealing with. Second, wisdom involves knowledge of the matters we are facing. The latter is the one the teacher mentioned in Proverbs 4. Similarly, in the book of Revelation, Apostle John wrote: "Here is wisdom. Let him that hath understanding count the number of the beast: for it is the number of a man; and his number is six hundred threescore and six" (Revelation 13:18).

A third way to spend money well is by taking care of our family. A man should work hard to support his family. To Timothy, Apostle Paul wrote, "But if any provide not for his own, and specially for those of his own house, he hath denied the faith, and is worse than an infidel" (1 Timothy 5:8). According to Paul, supporting our family is a major way our faith manifests. One might ask what the correlation is between supporting one's family and embracing the faith in Jesus Christ. Having compassion for others is at the center of Christianity, and failing to take care of our own family is a sign of a deranged heart. Furthermore, having work to take care of our family dignifies us. As men, it makes us proud to be able to give our wife and kids a place to live and other necessities.

It is possible for a woman to be so blessed financially that she doesn't really want a man to take care of her. In our modern age, social roles have evolved and we must consider that some changes can hurt the harmony of our families. How could the Bible say, for example, "the head of the woman is the man" (1 Corinthians 11:3) if the woman is already responsible to bear babies and support the household financially? It would be unfair to expect women to do both. Can a wealthy woman be respectful to a poor husband or a lazy one? It can sometimes be difficult to align the Word of God with socioeconomic situations in the age of modernity.

We must remind ourselves that in the past many women did not work. Now with the emancipation of the women in many regions, thanks in part to the feminist movement, they have professional careers with good wages and benefits. Women are smart, and many are lawyers, bankers, doctors, architects, senators, CEOs, and more. When your wife is making far more money than you do, how can you handle that without your ego exploding? The truth is, a lack of money from the husband can hurt a marriage as much as an excess from the wife can.

We see both outcomes in daily life and in our movies, as art often imitates reality. Many women must choose between their professional career and their family and, unfortunately, many save the former and lose the latter. But a Christian woman can save both with the wisdom from the Word of God. That's why it has to be all about love toward the object of your happiness: your spouse that you love for who he or she is. If a woman respects God and loves her husband, a well-paying job won't make her too arrogant to take her eyes off her money and title.

Alongside our family, we must also work to help others who might be in need. The Bible says: "Let him that stole steal no more: but rather let him labor, working with his hands the thing which is good, that he may have to give to him that needeth" (Ephesians 4:28). It is worth highlighting that according to this verse, one of the reasons I must work is to be able to help those in need. My work should first benefit others—or, at least, a source of benediction for others. The truth is, we must remember that we depend on the grace of God and not upon the work of our hands. God is the one who is going to bless his children. As Christians, it is a big mistake to rely so much upon our works, salary, and investments that we forget how God is their true source. We have to remember that God is the real provider of what we own, and to Him be the glory. We cannot react like the man in Jesus' parable:

> The ground of a certain rich man yielded an abundant harvest. He thought to himself, 'What should I do? I have no place to store my crops.' Then he said, 'This is what I'll do. I will tear down my barns and build bigger ones, and there I will store my surplus grain. And I'll say to myself, 'You have plenty of grain laid up for many years. Take life easy; eat, drink and be merry.' But God said to him, 'You fool! This very night your life will be demanded from you. Then who will get what you have prepared for yourself?' This is how it will be for whoever stores up things for themselves but is not rich toward God. (Luke 12:16–21 NIV)

This story is full of valuable lessons and characterizes the behavior of many in real life. First, notice how many times the rich man says "I"—five times in such a brief reflection. This is simply a description of a self-centered person. Sometimes we forget if family members struggle or if neighbors are in need. We frequently make it all about us instead. We sit at the table to eat a yummy dinner without thanking God or without thinking about the many families who, unlike us, have nothing to eat.

The man in Luke forgot that God is the author of the life he was enjoying. He couldn't have it or enjoy any wealth if His creator asks for it back. The best attitude would be to thank God for the gift of life and give back to the house of the Lord. We often rely too much upon what we have in our bank account when the grace of God covers everything. We think that our money is king and can save us from all kinds of situations. We are wrong, and it is time to keep our eyes upon God. It is better to be rich toward God or for the cause of God, as Jesus clearly expressed it after telling his parable: "This is how it will be for whoever stores up things for themselves but is not rich toward God" (Luke 12:21 NIV).

How does your money serve God's kingdom? What do you give to the house of the Lord? How do you help those in need? What type of seed did you plant in the ground? When our days end here on Earth and we are about to step into eternity, what exactly will we take with us? Our house or our car? No. Our wealth or our Individual Retirement Arrangement (IRA)? No. Only our sense of justice and our compassion will follow us, although this won't be the criteria for our salvation, which comes through faith in Jesus Christ by grace. According to the book of Ephesians, "For it is by grace you have been saved, through faith—and this is not from yourselves, it is the gift of God—not by works, so no one can boast" (Ephesians 2:8–9 NIV).

But any compensation—or "crown," to use a biblical term—will be a result of our work and our attitudes toward our brothers and the Church of God. One of the strongest arguments for this theological standpoint is found in 1 Corinthians:

> For no one can lay any foundation other than the one already laid, which is Jesus Christ. If anyone builds on this foundation using gold, silver, costly stones, wood, hay or straw, their work will be shown for what it is, because the Day will bring it to light. It will be revealed with fire, and the fire will test the quality of each person's work. If what has been built survives, the builder will receive a reward. If it is burned up, the builder will suffer loss but yet will be saved—even though only as one escaping trough the flames. (1 Corinthians 3:11–15 NIV)

It is useful to distinguish between our salvation, by grace through faith, and our rewards, which come from our works. Three people could be part of a kingdom, but each of them finds him or herself in a different room with a distinct place of honor. Finding salvation doesn't mean you will receive all the privileges in the kingdom of God. One of the judgments we read about in the Bible is the judgment of a believer's works Paul refers to in his letter to the Roman Church: "So then every one of us shall give account of himself to God" (Romans 14:12).

Our financial failure could be because, like Richardson and the prodigal son, we made some bad decisions and strayed from our Father. We spent our money unwisely. But our failure could also be because we lack blessings from God. If you do not plant any seeds, you cannot expect any harvest in return. That is simply a law of nature. If your heart desires to plant seeds, then God will give you more to plant and your harvest will be large. As the Word of God teaches us, "Now he who supplies seed to the sower and bread for food will also supply and increase your store of seed and will enlarge the harvest of your righteousness" (2 Corinthians 9:10 NIV). Remember one of the central lessons of Christianity: "It is more blessed to give than to receive" (Acts 20:35).

If you face financial failure because you spend your money foolishly, like Richardson and the prodigal son, I am here to let you know that God is willing to give you another chance to become financially independent. Even if your bad investments pushed you to poverty's limits, God can still help you rebuild your finances. Do not think about killing yourself. Money comes and money goes, but the Word and love of God will endure forever. Being spiritually healthy is more valuable than finances, and God can allow you to regain what you have lost. If you feel you are not blessed because you don't give what you should to the house of the Lord, I want to tell you that God is willing to give you another chance.

Our Lord is not a "Godfather" who punishes those who are supposed to give Him money for protection but don't show up. God simply wants you to believe in Him. He wants you to plant some financial seeds in His house and put your faith to work. He requests that you would be generous to those in need. He wishes for you to experience Him in a different way, that you would receive His infinite blessing, like He said to the People of Israel: "'Bring the whole tithe into the storehouse, that there may be food in my house. Test me in this,' says the LORD Almighty, 'and see if I will not throw open the floodgates of heavens and poor out so much blessing that there will not be room enough to store it'" (Malachi 3:10 NIV).

Another Chance for Your Broken Family

*And Adam gave names to all cattle, and to the fowl of the air,
and to every beast of the field; but for Adam there was not
found an help meet for him. (Genesis 2:20)*

*Call it a clan, call it a network, call it a tribe, call it a family:
whatever you call it, whoever you are, you need one.[10]
(Jane Howard)*

Family is without a doubt one of the most important assets
someone owns, although it can also be a liability. Life
often offers this duality: the object of our greatest happiness
can simultaneously be our greatest sadness. But in a perfect
world—or, at best, a world where we maintain our sense of
morality—family is sacred. Even if someone owns a large
amount of money, life can quickly seem meaningless without
a close group of people to share it with. We love to work hard

---

10. Jane Howard, *A Different Woman*. New York City: Dutton
1973.

to succeed financially and offer our loved ones the comfort we think they deserve.

Our parents gave us life and raised us. We spend time with and mutually support our siblings. We consider our spouses to be our other half, and we see our kids as an extension of our existence. All of these people constitute this group that we call family. A sociological point of view states that "a family is a socially recognized group- usually join by blood, marriage, cohabitation, and adoption- that forms an emotional connection and serves as an economic unit of society."[11] There is also a more restrictive type of family that sociologists call the "nuclear family," which can be defined as "a type of family unit that consists of two parents and their child(ren) who lived apart from their extended family."[12]

Both kinds of family are valuable, and the Bible refers to each of them. For example, when the Old Covenant mentions "the family of Jacob," it refers to Jacob, his wives, their kids— Joseph and his eleven brothers—and their wives. They were a group of people related by blood and marriage. In the New Covenant, Paul wrote to Timothy, "But if any [a man, to be exact] provide not for his own, and specially for those of his own house, he hath denied the faith, and is worse than an infidel" (1 Timothy 5:8). It is not an exaggeration to assume "those of his own house" refers to his wife and kids since the distinction of "his own" has already been made. Remember, Paul referred to family as husband, wife, and kids. To the Ephesian Church, he wrote, "Wives, submit yourselves unto your own husbands, as unto the Lord. . . . Husbands, love your wives, even as Christ also loved the church, and gave himself for it. . . . Children, obey your parents in the Lord:

---

11. Donna Giuliani, *Sociology of Family*. United States: Press-books, 2016.

12. Nicholas Abercrombie et al., *The Penguin Dictionary of Sociology*. United States: Penguin Books, 2006.

for this is right" (Ephesians 5:22–25; 6:1). The specificity in his language shows the nuclear aspect of a family.

By saying "It is not good that the man [Adam] should be alone" (Genesis 2:18), God became the first one to express the idea that "no man is an island"[13] in its original form. Having a spouse who you love is the best feeling ever. Raising your kids in a lovely, familial environment is the best experience ever. In both cases, our lives are more illuminated. Loneliness is our worst enemy. Finding ourselves in a beautiful mansion without another soul feels empty, like Adam living in paradise but sharing this "lack of form and void" Genesis 1:2 speaks to: a "tohu-bohu" of existence.

Communicating with others is one of the most important characteristics of the human condition. Despite facing the most beautiful flowers, the cleanest rivers, and unlimited riches, Adam was unable to truly express himself while alone. Who we address is a sine qua non for effective communication, and they can shape our form of communication or inspire its content. Without Eve, Adam could go insane. There are many other reasons why it is not good for Adam or any other man to be alone, as well.

It is worth noting that only after Eve was created did the Bible show Adam speaking expressively. If he had already named the animals, nothing was important enough to be reported. With Eve at his side, he mastered language like a poet: "This is now bone of my bones, and flesh of my flesh, she shall be called woman, because she was taken out of man" (Genesis 2:23). Now that he wasn't alone, he became happier and more communicative. Even in the most beautiful kingdom, something valuable is missing without our families.

---

13. John Donne, "Meditation XVII." In *Devotions upon Emergent Occasions*. London: Worshipful Company of Stationers, 1624.

Although Joseph's brothers sold him into slavery, he still enjoyed being around his family as Prime Minister for the Egyptian Pharaoh. The unchangeable truth was that those traitors were his brothers. How could he be happy in a kingdom with the most delicious food and the most beautiful women—two things that could make any man happy— while his family was living in a faraway country where there was a great famine? Joseph forgave his brothers and asked them to rejoin him in Egypt with their father, Jacob (Genesis 39–50). Sometimes bad events take place in our families, but at the end of the day, family is forever. Your brother will always be your brother although he stays far away and never exchanges a word; your sister will always be your sister even if she missed Thanksgiving and Christmas. Family is sacred, and one day everybody might sit around the same table and give thanks to God, as it was in the case of Joseph and his brothers. This powerful story teaches us we can forgive others for our mental liberation and constructive happiness.

We need to be a part of a family. We need to love and to be loved unconditionally. In this modern age, love is frequently confused with interest. Instead of being loved as a person, being loved for who we are, we can be "loved" for what we own. This is a situation where *eros* itself is under assault. We need people who will stay by our side when illness comes. People who sincerely take our hands while we are about to cross into eternity. People who give us a place in their hearts forever and ever. Family is a place where we often find that kind of person, who happens to be our parents, spouses, kids, siblings, or aunts and uncles.

Family was the first institution created by God Himself. Family is the center of each society and the core of each local church. When families are dysfunctional, our society becomes morally bankrupt and our churches become weak, losing their influence over the community. There is a good reason why the devil has attacked this institution from the beginning.

As a young married man, Richardson chose a path of destruction with some bad friends who took him away from his wife and his young kid. They pushed him far from the teaching of his lovely mother. He started to see all kind of imperfections in his beautiful and exemplary wife, Linda. He didn't spend enough time with his family and became irrational and angry for no reason. His wife even learned about his adultery and filed for divorce. The first three years of marriage have been like hell.

Like Richardson, if you feel you are about to lose your family, I'm here to let you know there is another chance through Jesus Christ. Your family is important to you. God wants you to do your best to save your family. He wants to help you rebuild the walls of morality that had fallen. Some battles are best won when we fall to our knees. Remember to pray to God and ask Him to change the circumstances through His profound grace—amazing grace! Just ask God for another chance, and your family would be saved. Amen.

8

Another Chance for Your Incurable Illness

As soon as they left the synagogue, they went with James and John to the home of Simon and Andrew. Simon's mother-in-law was in bed with a fever, and they immediately told Jesus about her. So he went to her, took her hand and helped her up. The fever left her and she began to wait on them. (Mark 1:29–31 NIV)

Illness is one of our greatest enemies, and it reminds us that we are fragile humans. During His ministry, Jesus healed many sick people. Among them was Simon's mother-in-law, who had a fever. Jesus wants to heal us from our illnesses, curable or incurable. If He was willing to give His own life for us, then He can do this, too.

Our body—a complex, imperfect machine—always needs healing from God via His Son, Jesus Christ. Richardson, for instance, was born surrounded by a thousand doctors. He neither cried nor breathed, a sign that something was wrong. After a long time, though, the doctors heard a weak sound, as if Richardson didn't have enough strength to cry. He had to stay at the hospital for a few days after that since he had faced so many health complications.

His mother had a simple phrase to sum up his condition: "Richardson is a miracle." She had to make sure her boy kept his asthma pump with him all the time, and when the spring season came, the flowers kept Richard coughing. His mother also had to be careful with her boy's food allergies. After her passing, Richardson found himself in a bad position since the lovely hand that used to separate the good from the bad in terms of foods and habits was gone. The authoritative, but graceful voice that used to tell him to take his medicine was no more. Only an emptiness remained. But like Hugo beautifully wrote "the mind as well as the nature abhors all forms of emptiness."[14] Other voices, like the one of his lovely fiancée, tried to help him. Another hand tried to remind him that he must take care of his health. But no one can replace a lovely mother. No other voice has power like our mothers'. Being with his friend, who just did not care about his illnesses, made things worse.

The truth is, God wants us to be healthy. He said to the people of Israel, "I am the LORD, who heals you" (Exodus 15:26 NIV). He is a compassionate God, and He simply did not wish the same illnesses that would destroy the Egyptians to kill the Israelites. Illness is not from God. We often become ill because our body is imperfect without the Spirit of God in it. "Remember the Lord long said: My Spirit shall not always strive with man, for that he also is flesh, yet his days shall be a one hundred and twenty" (Genesis 6:3). The moral deterioration of the human race incited God to limit the numbers of days man would live. Alongside physical death, illnesses come into the equation because man is simply flesh, and flesh without a good spirit is just a fragile object. That is

---

14. Victor Hugo, *The Man Who Laughs*. United States: Create Space, 2015.

why Christians in the presence of the Holy Spirit are often healed.

Death usually follows illness, but the good news is God says He can heal us. Throughout His ministry, Jesus healed so many people because he also came to save us from our broken state. Today He can heal you, too. Apostle John wrote to Gaius, a faithful leader of one or multiple churches in Asia Minor, "Dear friend, I pray that you may enjoy good health and that all may go well with you, even as your soul is getting along well" (3 John 1:2 NIV). Apostle John knew that we cannot fully serve God if we are not healthy. Someone could own billions of dollars and many beautiful mansions and luxurious cars, but if he or she is not healthy to enjoy life, everything they own is in vain.

If, like Richardson, your body dwells with many illnesses, I'm here to tell you that God can heal you. He wants to give you another chance. Some of you might have cancer, but God can heal you. Doctors may tell you that you won't make it, but God still can heal you. How many people have been told by their physicians they would die but are still alive today? The word of a doctor is the word of a man. This might be the word of science, but it is not the Word of God. God has the final word, and He is above all science and nature. All you have to do is believe in God and open your heart.

9

Put Your Sin in Your Past as God Has Already Done

As far as the east is from the west, so far has He removed our transgressions from us. As a father has compassion on his children, so the LORD has compassion on those who fear Him; for He knows how we are formed, He remembers that we are dust. (Psalm 103:12–14 NIV)

Blessed are those whose transgressions are forgiven, whose sins are covered. (Romans 4:7 NIV)

At least once in our lives, many of us have sinned and—even after asking God for forgiveness with a repentant heart—wondered if we were really forgiven. If it is a recurring sin, we think sometimes God won't even look at us while we're on our knees crying out, asking for strength that comes from above. Let me emphasize that a sense of perpetual guilt is the devil's work and, unfortunately, many people experience it. Satan wants Christians to believe that they are bad people because they sin today. He wants you to think you're a piece of garbage since you committed the same sin last month and will do so again in the future.

If we see ourselves as bad Christians, we might become comfortable in our sin, especially the sin that we are fighting. Each believer has strengths and weaknesses. Apostle James expresses this idea of faulty nature when he wrote, "We all stumble in many ways. Anyone who is never at fault in what they say is perfect, able to keep their whole body in check" (James 3:2 NIV). The last person to be surprised by James's words is God Himself because He knows how we are formed. The Lord isn't shocked by our sins because He remembers that we are dust.

In His compassion and great understanding, God decided to put our transgressions as far as the east is from the west. That is great news because if sinners were held responsible for their own sins, they would deserve death. Consequently, "Blessed are those whose transgressions are forgiven, whose sins are covered" (Psalm 32:1 NIV). If we ask God for forgiveness with a repentant heart and He forgives us, we hurt ourselves spiritually when we ask if we have really been forgiven. We misunderstand God's mercy and power.

The devil is very pleased when we do this because his goal is that we see ourselves as slaves to sin. He surely enjoys it when we live with a constant sense of guilt. He wants us to believe we belong to him. But it is not true. Just because we sin doesn't mean we are not really Christians. As I already stated, we all have our flaws. Even habitual sin doesn't mean we are not Christians. It simply means we must be more careful about our state of mind leading into this mischief. It means we must be quick to act. It might be useful to spend more time on our knees to ask God for more strength through the sacrifice of His Son, Jesus Christ. There is no sin that His blood cannot wash away.

On the other hand, it is worth noting that sanctification happens progressively, unlike the justification that happens the moment we invite God to come into our heart. Apostle Paul wrote to the Church of Corinth, "Therefore, since we have these promises, dear friends, let us purify ourselves from everything that contaminates body and spirit, perfecting holiness out of reverence for God" (2 Corinthians 7:1 NIV). Sanctification is to be perfected or worked on each and every day.

A theological question on hamartiology—the doctrine of sin—evidently arises: do believers have some sin in their hearts even after they are saved? The short answer is yes. Apostle Paul clearly says:

> I do not understand what I do. For what I want to do I do not do, but what I hate I do. And if I do what I do not want to do, I agree that the law is good. As it is, it is no longer I myself who do it, but it is sin living in me. For I know that good itself does not dwell in me, that is, in my sinful nature, For I have the desire to do what is good, but I cannot carry it out. (Romans 7:15–18 NIV)

Along with Peter, James, and John, Paul is one of the most important members of Christianity. What he expresses here is the powerful impact of our old, sinful identities, which are still present even after we truly become Christians through baptism in the Holy Spirit. At this time, the old nature has not disappeared but is mastered or controlled.

In his conclusion, Paul asks who will deliver him from his old sin nature, and he answers himself by saying, "Thanks to be God, who delivers me through Jesus Christ our Lord!" (Romans 7:25 NIV). A Christian will be totally free from sin only when he or she is in the presence of the Lord in heaven or wherever Christ might be. One might ask what Jesus meant when He told His disciples, "So if the Son sets you free, you will be free indeed" (John 8:36 NIV). As powerful as our old sin nature might be, we are no longer enslaved to sin because of the power of Jesus Christ's sacrifice, which frees us. We do not embrace any sin. We do not become comfortable with any sin. And any sin is a sin to ask God to forgive and abandon thereafter.

Our old nature is not an excuse to become comfortable in our mischief, nor should we use the love and grace of God as a tent to hide in so we can continue committing sins. We would be wrong to try to justify any sin in our life. Rather we should be willing to give up any form of sin with the power of the Holy Spirit and the shedding of the blood of Jesus. If we meet Christ one day and we confess His name, receiving the Holy Spirit, we won't feel comfortable sinning without resistance or regret. The fear of God won't allow that. Paul asked this important question to the Roman Church: "We are those who have died to sin; how can we live in it any longer?" (Romans 6:2 NIV).

Because of our old nature, we may sin almost every day of our lives. A Christian might commit a sin, but he isn't living in a continual state of sin like a nonbeliever. He also might have a specific sin he is fighting. Because of the power of the Holy Spirit living in us, we can say "no" to the evil voices in our head. But if we sin, we must ask God for forgiveness with a sincere heart and a desire not to sin again and put it in our past. The devil wants to use our past mistakes to compromise our present walk with God. Do not ask if God really forgives you; He does. He sent your sins as far as the east is from the west. He is more than happy to give you another chance because His love endures eternally.

Go, and Sin No More: An Invitation to Separate Your Past from Your Present

No love can compare to the love of God. We could change all the world's rivers and seas into ink and all the trees into pens. Yet this immense amount of ink would not be enough to express this love in writing, as an old Christian song meaningfully says.[15] The infinite grace of God has been manifested through Jesus Christ. I cannot imagine how shocked religious leaders were when they heard about how an adulterous woman had been saved from spiritual death by a man who pretended to be the Son of God. A man whose father was a simple carpenter, whose brother and sisters lived in the village of Nazareth without any social recognition.

"Go, and sin no more" was an invitation for the adulterous woman to separate her past from her present and

_____

15. Frederick Lehman, *The Love of God*. Chicago: Light and Life Press, 1917.

receive salvation through Jesus Christ. This was an invitation to come abide in the light of the world, which is Jesus Christ, who unequivocally stated, "I am the light of the world. Whoever follows me will never walk in darkness, but will have the light of life" (John 8:12 NIV). When Jesus speaks to one of us, He really speaks to all of us; indeed, "go, and sin no more" is an invitation for each of us to stop doing bad things and start doing good deeds.

Unfortunately some people reject this invitation, and they live a life where yesterday's bad habits repeat today and tomorrow. They disregard the opportunity to be washed by Jesus' blood by believing and receiving Him in their hearts. It is not a difficult decision. Jesus said, "Take my yoke upon you and learn from me, for I am gentle and humble in heart, and you will find rest for your souls. For my yoke is easy and my burden is light" (Matthew 11:29–30 NIV). His yoke is easy because we simply need to do God's will through the commands of Jesus Christ and let Him guide our life. We only need to obey because we believe. The yoke is light compared to the harsh requirements of the Mosaic Law.

On the other hand, some of us have had a troublesome life and, having asked God for forgiveness with a repentant heart, need to be separated from our past since God forgave us once and for all. Do not embrace a sense of perpetual guilt, which will hurt your spiritual journey with God. Stop asking yourself if you are really forgiven because there is no sin that the blood of Jesus cannot wash away.

Additionally let us do our best to give every part of our lives to the Lord. Let us take a firm stand to serve the Lord faithfully. Let us not be like the Corinthians, to whom Paul said He could only give them spiritual milk because they were not mature enough for solid food (1 Corinthians 3:1–4). As Christians, we often continue to practice old habits that keep our spiritual life in disarray. We love God, but we are not placing our entire lives on the altar. It doesn't matter what we used to do it is all about this conviction to sin no more.

Richardson finally came back to the Church of God in Flora County where he grew up, a place that held countless memories of his lovely mother. His brothers and sisters in Christ were so happy to see him again in the house of the Lord, and Pastor Andrew was pleased to see his brother and his friend back. He had told himself again and again that his prayers in favor of Richardson would not be in vain and that God would make a way because He could finish what He had started. His spiritual Father in heaven must have celebrated with the angels the same way the father of the prodigal son did when his son had come back home.

Richardson took back his guitar and sang as he used to do so before. His wife forgave him, and the couple was so happy together. He saved his family. No more drugs, no more alcohol, no more smoking. His health has improved since his wife has been keeping an eye on him. The couple has also been blessed financially thanks to a new asthma medicine they created, for which a patent has been approved (Richardson's wife Linda has a medical background). They even went to Shark Tank and have been offered a deal. God gave Richardson another chance on so many levels, and He is willing to do the same for you because He is the God of second chances.

When it comes to the forgiven adulteress, we do not have any more information about her after this event. What we do know is that anyone who meets with Jesus will never be the same. Surely she listened to the call of Jesus to sin no more.

When Jesus comes into our hearts, something's got to change. When we profess the name of Jesus, we are not slaves of sin anymore. Like the Samaritan woman, we should go let others know about our experience with Jesus (John 4:28–29). We should be glad to inform them that we found a Prophet different from other prophets. A Father unlike our human fathers. A God distinct from other gods.

Whatever sin you've committed, God is willing to forgive you if you repent with all your heart and agree to be transformed by the power of the Holy Spirit. You must separate your past from your present, using it only to instruct you.

God is willing to give you another chance in any situation you might find yourself. Today's society would be glad to see you condemned, like the Jewish accusers who sought to stone the adulterous woman. But Jesus, with His head bowed, wrote on the ground. Maybe he said, "I bring her grace, I bring her love, and I bring her forgiveness." If I'm wrong in my guess, thank God I'm right in what the Gospel teaches us: that Jesus came with this beautiful bouquet of flowers made with grace, love, and forgiveness. He wants to tell you today, "Neither do I condemn thee: go, and sin no more" (John 8:11).